COURAGE

Written by

Marie C. Marsh

Illustrated by

Stephen Adams

AuthorHouse™
1663 Liberty Drive
Bloomington, IN 47403
www.authorhouse.com
Phone: 1-800-839-8640

First published by AuthorHouse   07/11/2011

ISBN: 978-1-4634-0167-2

Library of Congress Control Number: 2011908214

Printed in the United States of America

Any people depicted in stock imagery provided by Thinkstock are models,
and such images are being used for illustrative purposes only.
Certain stock imagery © Thinkstock.

This book is printed on acid-free paper.

Because of the dynamic nature of the Internet, any web addresses or links contained in this book may have changed
since publication and may no longer be valid. The views expressed in this work are solely those of the author and do not
necessarily reflect the views of the publisher, and the publisher hereby disclaims any responsibility for them.

authorHOUSE®

This book is dedicated to my son, LCDR Robert J. Marsh USNR and the brave men and women that serve beside him.

Special thanks to my husband, Dennis and daughter, Jessica for their love and support.

Puppies come into our lives at all different times. Some are expected and, sometimes, very unexpected. There are Christmas puppies, all dressed up in big red bows. There are birthday puppies, and "I love you" puppies. There are puppies that just seem to find you, even when you are not looking for one. Puppies teach us many things. Loving someone all the time and being faithful is a strong lesson a puppy can teach us. There are times in our lives when only the love of a puppy can fill an empty place in your heart. Puppies love you and never let you forget that you are their best friend!

This is the story of Courage.

Somewhere in the Midwest there was a special place called Holly Farm. It was a beautiful farm, with green rolling hills. It was spring, and the farm pastures were filled with grazing cows. The newborn calves stayed very close to their mothers. Horses ran free—their manes and tails blowing in the soft breeze. The colts ran and played among themselves. After a long play, they could be found in the tall grass, fast asleep in the warm spring sun. With the spring came all the other baby animals. The farm, after a very long, hard winter, was alive with new life.

In the distance, voices rang out. It was Kelly calling, "Renee, the third one is being born." Renee rushed in to see the last of a litter of puppies making a grand entrance into the world. It was a little boy puppy. He was gray, with black markings. He had big eyes, with black circles around them. He looked just like his two other sisters. They were so tiny! Frosty, the father of the litter, watched as Brooke nuzzled her puppies. She was trying to get them to nurse, and she was so very tired. Kelly and Renee had been up all night with Brooke. They wanted to make sure all the puppies were delivered safely. "They are a beautiful litter," Renee said. "It will be hard for us to let them go when they are weaned." It was always hard to part with the puppies. Kelly and Renee always loved them.

The coming days brought delight for everyone to see. The puppies grew bigger with each new day. Their little eyes began to open. The puppies' little legs grew stronger. Playtime was fun to watch, as they rolled around and jumped all over each other. Having that much fun made them tired. The next time you looked, they were all nestled around each other, sound asleep.

In what seemed to be no time at all, they were six weeks old and ready to go to new homes. The female puppies had been sold to a farmer nearby. Renee had made arrangements for someone to take the little boy puppy. "Kelly, this little guy is going to New York. There is a puppy store that wants him." Kelly agreed.

They knew that the time for good-byes was here. The female puppies went to a home where there were lots of children to love them. A very nice man called Harry came to the farm to pick up the last puppy. "I will take good care of him for you," he said. Kelly and Renee gave the puppy hugs and kisses, and he was on his way.

The little pup slept most of the trip. When he was awake, he would think, *It is lonely without my sisters to play with.* He missed his mom and dad very much. Harry checked on him often to make sure he was okay. Finally, after a few days, they arrived at the puppy store. It was in a quaint little coastal town, with lots of visitors who came there by ferry. Harry got out of the truck and took the puppy with him. Liz, the owner of the store, greeted him. "Is this the puppy from Kelly and Renee?"

"Yes," said Harry. Liz took the puppy and put him in a huge cage with lots of soft paper on the bottom. He looked around at all the other puppies. *They are just like me,* he thought.

As the days went by, the little puppy made friends with the others. They all played together, rolling all over each other, and biting each others' ears until they were tired. Then, in a quick flash, they were fast asleep. The daily visitors to the puppy store kept them entertained. There were always a lot of children wanting to touch them. *So many faces looking at me*, the little puppy thought. Some of his friends were bought and taken to new homes. *It seems like I have been here forever. I wonder if someone will take me home too,* thought the little puppy.

Not far away lived a family who was planning a big going-away party for their son, Lt. Mike. He was a navy officer. Lt. Mike lived far away from his family, but he had come home to visit his mom and dad and little sister, Faith. He would be leaving at the end of the week for a distant land called Iraq. He wanted to be with his family before he left. His mom and dad had invited family and friends from all over the country to see him. They came to give good wishes to this brave young man. His family wanted to send him off with lots of love and fond memories of those who cared about him. The huge party went as planned, and family and friends came to see Lt. Mike. His grandparents came, as well as aunts, uncles, and cousins. Little Joshua sang the song, "She's a Grand Old Flag" for Lt. Mike. It was a wonderful time for everyone!

The week ahead was filled with lots of fun events. There were all sorts of day trips, including the beautiful day the family took a ride to a little coastal town. As Lt. Mike and Faith were walking down the street, they suggested to Mom and Dad that they make a quick stop at the puppy store. "Sure, why not?" said Dad. Lt. Mike wanted to get a puppy when he got back to the States. They walked in the store, and the little puppy stopped playing to stare at them. *I like that family,* he thought. Lt. Mike and his family looked at all the puppies. *I don't think that they even noticed me. I guess I am not for them.*

Days passed, and the little puppy saw that family again. This time, something was different. Faith and Lt. Mike were pointing to some of the puppies. Liz was taking them out of the cages and putting them into cribs so Faith and Lt. Mike could play with them. "They are so cute!" said Faith.

"You all need a dog in the house!" said Lt. Mike. Mom and Dad pointed to the little puppy, and Liz put him in the crib also.

"He is very cute," said Mom.

Faith asked, "Mom, can't we get him?"

The little puppy heard Mom say, "Honey, a puppy is like having a baby in the house. We are so busy. How would we have time to care for him? He is adorable, but now might not be the right time." *I think they do like me*, thought the puppy as his little tail wagged. But it was not the right time for them. Liz put him back in the cage. He was so disappointed. *I really want to go home with them and be part of their family*, thought the little puppy.

Lt. Mike and his family spent the rest of the week together. As the week came to an end, it got harder and harder for his family, knowing he would be leaving soon. But, they knew he had a very special job to do.

It was Friday morning, and the puppy store was packed with people, especially children. It was the first day of summer vacation, and the town was bustling. Gina, another lady who cared for the puppies, came to the cage where the little puppy slept. "Okay, little guy, someone is coming for you! We are going to give you a bath and make you soft." After his bath, he had a big red bow put around his neck.

A young man carried him out to meet his new family. *It is them! It is the family that I want to go home with. They chose me!* He was so happy, so very happy. The young man handed him over to Faith, and she hugged him. Lt. Mike patted him on the head. Mom took the puppy from Faith and kissed him. "We want you to be part of our family now. We are going to call you Courage. We will always think of Lt. Mike when we call your name." Courage very happily went home with his new family. Later that day, Lt. Mike left for Iraq.

Courage changed their lives. He came to them at a time when they needed his love. Lt. Mike called as much as he could to see how Courage was doing. His family spent lots of time with Courage, training him so he would someday be a good citizen. *They all really love me,* thought Courage. *Mom tells me every day how I helped them all get through one of the hardest times of their lives.*

Courage continued to grow and learn, and nine months later, Lt. Mike came home.

ABOUT THE AUTHOR

Marie C. Marsh, graduate of the French Fashion Academy in New York City, New York is a mother of two grown children. As all parents know, you take on the job of a doctor, counselor, coach, teacher, vet, religion teacher and everything else when you are raising children. It was her personal experience as the mother of a Navy officer that helped in writing this book. The emotions of parting with her son leaving to go to Iraq prompted her to put in words what helped her get through this event. Thus, "COURAGE" was written. It is her intentions that perhaps her experience can help other children and parents coping with the same issues.

Marie Marsh has worked in the general dentistry field for 37 years .The past 16 years, and most exciting, she has worked for a cosmetic dentistry practice helping people to feel good about themselves. She truly loves the experience of working with people every day. Mrs. Marsh also served her church along with her husband, Dennis in different ministries. She also has volunteered for several charitable organizations as well as Treasurer and Board Member for a local Chamber of Commerce.

A native to Long Island, New York, Marie Marsh lives with her husband, Dennis of 37 years and her daughter, Jessica.

Marie Marsh can be reached at mcmCourage@yahoo.com

CPSIA information can be obtained
at www.ICGtesting.com
Printed in the USA
246729LV00004B

YELLOW ELEPHANT
A BRIGHT BESTIARY

Poems by Julie Larios

Paintings by Julie Paschkis

HARCOURT, INC.   ORLANDO   AUSTIN   NEW YORK   SAN DIEGO   TORONTO   LONDON

Library of Congress
Cataloging-in-Publication Data
Larios, Julie Hofstrand, 1949–
Yellow elephant/Julie Larios;
illustrated by Julie Paschkis.
p. cm.
1. Animals—Juvenile poetry.
2. Colors—Juvenile poetry.
3. Children's poetry, American.
I. Paschkis, Julie. II. Title.
PS3562.A7233Y45 2006
811'.54—dc22   2004025163
ISBN-13: 978-0152-05422-9
ISBN-10: 0-15-205422-7

First edition
H G F E D C B A

Manufactured in China

The illustrations in this book were done in
gouache on Arches paper.

The display and text type were set in
Worcester Round.

Color separations by Colourscan Co. Pte. Ltd.,
Singapore

Manufactured by South China Printing
Company, Ltd., China

This book was printed on totally chlorine-free
Stora Enso Matte paper.

Production supervision by Ginger Boyer

Designed by Linda Lockowitz

For Fernando
—J. L.

For Stephen Iino
—J. P.

C O N T E N T S

GREEN FROG

One thing for sure
about a green frog
on a green lily pad
on a green day
in spring:
One hop
and her green
is gone.
See how she swims,
blue frog now
under blue water.

4

RED DONKEY

Red clay road.
Red donkey braying.
He has a red temper.
He's probably saying,
This load is too heavy.
I'm hungry.
My feet hurt!
I'm tired!
I'm hot!
It's
not
fair!
Red donkey sits down.
Someone shouts, "Come!"
But he won't come.
Red donkey tantrum.

7

WHITE OWL

Who?
asks the white owl,
all eyes.
Who?
This is his riddle.
In the world's white weather,
who has white feathers?
Who flies over white ice?
Who?
And over white snow?
Who flies while the white wind blows?

ORANGE GIRAFFE

Orange sun rising
over the savanna—
can you see the orange water
of the Juba River?
Can you hear the hyena's
high orange laugh?
Look!
On the riverbank,
an orange giraffe.

YELLOW ELEPHANT

Yellow elephant
in the jungle sun,
in the day's yellow heat,
trumpeting her song
and galumphing along.
Oh,
I think no other animal can
(I know a mosquito can't)
glow in the jungle sun
like a wild-eared
yellow elephant.

13

PURPLE PUPPY

Purple ball for the puppy.
He's feeling pretty nippy.
Needs to run, maybe.
Chases purple birds
and furry squirrels—
he's zigging, they're zagging.
Puppy tail wags.
Now he drinks cool water
with his purple tongue
slurping.

PINK KITTY

Pink collar.
Pink bell.
Pink pillow.
Pink bowl.
And a pink yawn at dawn.
Outside, the city—hot and hazy.
Inside, cool kitty
feeling pink and lazy.

BLACK FISH

Now all silver quiver.
Now all dark flash.
She's all water and wonder,
this black fish.

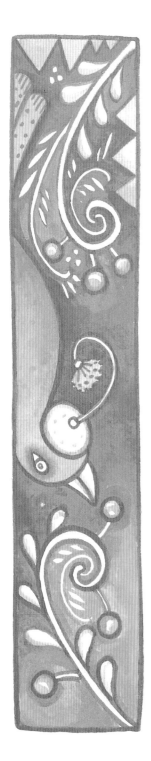

GOLD FINCH

Clinging to a prickly thistle,
the gold finch flutters, whistles,
then flies away.
Some say
his song is only as long
as his tail feathers,
three gold notes
that float.

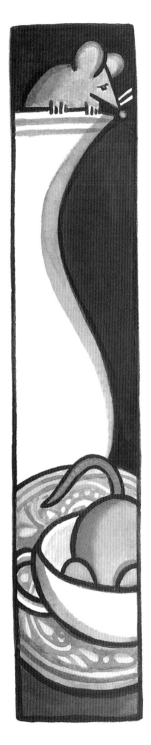

BROWN MOUSE

Little brown clown,
looking for crumbs,
comes sneaking, sniffing, skittering
all around—sounds
like she's jitterbugging
on tinfoil, sharp toenails
clicking and clacking
through the house.
She's in a hurry,
that's for sure,
this brown mouse.

SILVER GULL

Silver gull
on a cedar pole
in the salt water
sees a silver heron
with his beady eyes on the tide.
Summer fog
hides the birds, hides the boulders,
hides the silver beach logs.

TURQUOISE LIZARD

Thunder rolls
across the desert,
quieting the buzz
of the cicadas.
One worried lizard
zips quickly
under a rock.
When raindrops fall,
the small lizard,
turquoise tail curled,
stays bright and dry
in the wet world.

BLUE TURTLE

Slow
in the blue shade
of a blue-leafed garden.
Slow
in the blue gloam.
Hard-shelled and unsudden,
the blue turtle in cool dirt,
heading home.

GRAY GOOSE

Gray mama goose
in a tizzy,
honk-honk-honking herself dizzy,
can't find her gosling,
she's honking and running,
webbed feet slapping,
all wild waddle,
her feathers a muddle,
splashing through puddles,
wings flapping. . . .

Ah,
there's her gold baby,
all fuzz,
napping.

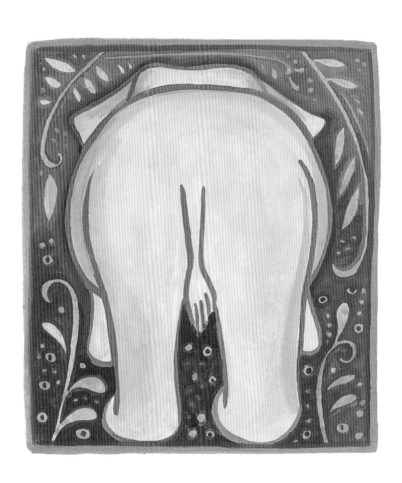